THE CIVIL WAR

History SparkNotes

SPARKNOTES is a registered trademark of SparkNotes LLC

Spark Educational Publishing
A Division of Barnes & Noble Publishing
120 Fifth Avenue
New York, NY 10011
www.sparknotes.com

ISBN 1-4114-0420-3

Please submit all comments and questions or report errors to *www.sparknotes.com/errors*.

Printed and bound in the United States

CONTENTS

OVERVIEW

The Civil War was certainly the most catastrophic event in American history. More than 600,000 Northerners and Southerners died in the war, a greater number than all those who had died in all other American wars combined. As many as 50,000 died in a single battle. The high death toll particularly hurt the South, which had a smaller population going into the war.

Nearly every American lost someone in the war: a friend, relative, brother, son, or father. In fact, the war was so divisive that it split some families completely in two. One U.S. senator, for example, had a son who served as a general in the Union army and another as a general for the Confederacy. Even the "Great Emancipator" Abraham Lincoln himself had four brothers-in-law who fought for the South.

As disastrous as the war was, however, it also brought the states—in the North as well as the South—closer together. After the war, the United States truly was *united* in every sense of the word. Most obvious, the war ended the debate over slavery that had divided North and South since the drafting of the Constitution in 1787. States had bickered over Missouri, the Wilmot Proviso and the Mexican Cession, Texas, California, the Fugitive Slave Laws, *Dred Scott v. Sanford*, Bleeding Kansas, and John Brown and had still been unable to resolve the dispute. In this sense, the Civil War had become inevitable once it was clear that compromises such as the three-fifths clause, the Missouri Compromise, and the Compromise of 1850 had little effect. With each decade, the two regions had drifted further and further apart. Lincoln's Emancipation Proclamation of 1863, however, ended the debate for good. Lincoln knew that only when slavery had been abolished would the debate end and the Union be reunited.

The Union victory also ended the debates over states' rights versus federalism. Southerners and Democrats had believed since Thomas Jefferson's and James Madison's Virginia and Kentucky Resolutions that states had the right to overrule the federal government when Congress acted unconstitutionally. In other words, they believed that states—not the Supreme Court—had the power of judicial review to determine whether Congress's laws were constitutional or unconstitutional. John C. Calhoun had raised this point in his *South Carolina Exposition and Protest* during the Nullification Crisis of the 1830s when he had urged his state to nullify the Tariff of Abominations. Whigs and Republicans, on the other hand, generally believed the opposite—that only the Supreme Court had the power of judicial review and that it was the duty of the states to obey the Court. The South's defeat asserted federal power over the states and settled the debate once and for all.

The Civil War was also a significant event in world history because the North's victory proved that democracy worked. When war broke out in 1861, many monarchs in Europe had believed smugly that the United States was on the brink of collapse. Democracy, they argued, was too volatile, too messy, and too fragile to be of any practical use. Lincoln himself recognized the historical significance of the war even before it was over. In his Gettysburg Address, he argued that the Civil War was a test for democracy and that the outcome of the war would determine the fate of representative government for the entire world. In his words, ". . . we here highly resolve . . . that government of the people, by the people, for the people, shall not perish from the earth."

Summary of Events

THE ELECTION OF 1848

Some historians have called the **Mexican War** the first battle of the Civil War, for it revived intense and heated debate about the expansion of slavery in the West. Tensions came to a head when Pennsylvanian congressman David Wilmot set forth the **Wilmot Proviso** in 1846, proposing that slavery be banned in the West. Not surprisingly, Southerners killed the proviso in the Senate before it could become law.

Nonetheless, the damage had been done, and expansion of slavery remained the hot topic in the **election of 1848**. The Whigs nominated war hero General **Zachary Taylor** on a rather noncommittal platform (they didn't want to lose Southern votes), while the Democrats nominated **Lewis Cass**. Hoping to appeal to voters from both regions, Cass proposed applying **popular sovereignty** to the slavery question, arguing that the citizens living in each territory should decide for themselves whether theirs would become a slave state or a free state. Taylor won the election, but he died after only sixteen months in office, and Vice President **Millard Fillmore** became president in 1850.

THE COMPROMISE OF 1850

Because Taylor and Fillmore had never made their views on slavery in the West clear, the issue remained unresolved. When California applied for admission as a free state, the debate picked up right where it had left off. In Congress, heavyweights **Daniel Webster** and **Henry Clay** met for the last time to hammer out a compromise. After much debate, the North and South finally came to an agreement that both sides thought would be lasting and binding.

There were five components to this **Compromise of 1850**. First, California would be admitted as a free state. Second, popular sovereignty would determine the fate of the other western territories. Third, Congress would cancel some of Texas's debts and, in exchange, give some of Texas's western land to New Mexico Territory. Fourth, slave trading would be banned in Washington, D.C. Finally, Congress would pass a tougher **Fugitive Slave Law**, to reduce the number of slaves who escaped to the North and Canada every year. Although Southerners had not conceded a lot in making the bargain, Northerners were still offended by the new law, and many refused to obey it.

PIERCE AND EXPANSION

The pro–Southern Democrat **Franklin Pierce** replaced Fillmore after defeating Whigs and Free-Soilers in the election of 1852. Playing off manifest destiny and the Southern desire for new slave states, Pierce supported a variety of proposals to acquire more territory. He tacitly supported adventurer **William Walker**'s attempt to annex Nicaragua but backed off after Walker was deposed and executed. Pierce also investigated the possible acquisition of Cuba from Spain, but the plan backfired after his machinations were leaked to Northerners in the **Ostend Manifesto**. More productively, he sent the U.S. Navy to Japan to open trade negotiations and bought a small strip of land in present-day Arizona and New Mexico in the 1853 **Gadsden Purchase**.

THE KANSAS-NEBRASKA ACT

Hoping to attract railroad development through the North, Illinois Senator **Stephen Douglas** introduced the **Kansas-Nebraska Act** in 1854 and pushed it successfully through Congress. The act carved the territory into the Kansas and Nebraska territories and, more controversially, declared that popular sovereignty would determine the future of slavery there.

THE DEATH OF THE MISSOURI COMPROMISE

Southerners jumped at this opportunity, because the act effectively repealed the **Missouri Compromise** of 1820 that had banned slavery north of the 36° 30' parallel. As soon as the Kansas-Nebraska Act passed, hundreds of Missourians crossed the state line into Kansas with their slaves to push for slavery. These **"border ruffians"** set up a government in Lecompton, Kansas, and rigged elections to get more proslavery delegates sent to the constitutional convention. Northerners were shocked and astonished that Southerners had managed to repeal the almost-sacred Missouri Compromise.

BLEEDING KANSAS

Fearing that Kansas would become the next slave state, hundreds of Northern abolitionists also flocked to the territory and set up their own government in Lawrence. A band of proslavery men, however, burned Lawrence to the ground in 1856. In revenge, an abolitionist gang led by **John Brown** killed five border ruffians at the **Pottawatomie Massacre**.

These two events sparked an internal war so savage that many referred to the territory as **"Bleeding Kansas."** The Kansas crisis was so shocking and so controversial that it even ignited tempers in

Washington, D.C. In the most infamous case, one Southern congressman nearly caned abolitionist Senator **Charles Sumner** to death on the Senate floor for speaking out against the act and its authors.

THE ELECTION OF 1856

Bleeding Kansas was the hottest topic in the presidential election of 1856. Democrat **James Buchanan** eventually defeated his Republican and Know-Nothing foes after many Southern states threatened to secede if a Republican became the next president. Just days after Buchanan took office, a new controversy hit: Chief Justice **Roger Taney**, along with a majority of the other justices of the Supreme Court, declared the Missouri Compromise unconstitutional in the 1857 *Dred Scott v. Sanford* decision. The ruling startled Northerners because it meant that slavery technically could no longer be banned *anywhere* in the United States.

THE BUCHANAN YEARS

Several states flat-out ignored the ruling, and Stephen Douglas challenged the Court when he proclaimed in his **Freeport Doctrine** during the **Lincoln-Douglas debates** that only popular sovereignty could decide the slavery question. But Buchanan backed Taney and also accepted the proslavery **Lecompton Constitution**, which border ruffians had drafted to make Kansas a new slave state. Douglas and others, however, blocked the constitution in the Senate.

Buchanan's presidency was also marred by **John Brown**'s attempt to incite a massive slave uprising by seizing the federal arsenal at Harpers Ferry, Virginia (in present-day West Virginia). The **Harpers Ferry Raid** went awry, however, and resulted only in Brown's capture. While Northerners mourned his execution, Southerners cheered.

THE ELECTION OF 1860

The **election of 1860** took place amid this supercharged atmosphere. The Republicans nominated **Abraham Lincoln,** who was morally opposed to slavery but wanted to maintain the Union above all else. Northern Democrats wanted Stephen Douglas to run, but Southerners in the party refused to back him after he betrayed the South by opposing the Lecompton Constitution. As a result, the party split: Northern Democrats nominated Douglas, while Southern Democrats nominated Vice President **John C. Breckinridge**. The **Constitutional Union Party**, a minor offshoot of the Republican Party, nominated **John Bell.**

Southerners again threatened to secede if a Republican was elected. On Election Day, Lincoln received 40 percent of the popular vote and more electoral votes than all the other candidates combined.

SECESSION

South Carolina made good on its threats and seceded from the Union shortly after Lincoln's election. Six other states soon followed. Together, they established a new government called the **Confederate States of America** in Richmond, Virginia, and chose **Jefferson Davis** as its first president. Four slave states, however, chose to remain in the Union. These **border states** proved invaluable to the North in the war.

In April 1861, Confederate forces attacked **Fort Sumter**, a Union stronghold in the harbor of Charleston, South Carolina. The Union forces fell after intense bombardment, and the Civil War had begun. Shortly after the battle, four more states seceded from the Union and joined the Confederacy.

STRENGTHS AND WEAKNESSES

Both sides initially believed the war would end quickly. The Union had greater population, a larger army, and a robust industrial economy. The Confederacy, however, thought it stood a good chance because it would be fighting a defensive war with better military commanders. The South also was confident that cotton-dependent Britain would take its side. Illusions of an easy victory vanished for both, however, after the **First Battle of Bull Run** in 1861 and the bloody **Battle of Shiloh** in 1862.

A STRONG FEDERAL GOVERNMENT

President Lincoln pushed the limits of the Constitution several times throughout the war, believing that desperate times called for desperate measures. He suspended the writ of **habeas corpus**, illegally increased the size of the army, and ordered a naval blockade of the South. The Supreme Court often objected, but Congress usually sided with Lincoln.

Congress itself took bold action by passing a series of progressive new laws such as the **Morrill Tariff**, the **Legal Tender Act**, and the **National Bank Act**. These acts helped industry and gave the federal government unprecedented control over the economy. A **draft** was also enacted to increase the size of the army, much to the consternation of poorer Americans. Protests and riots, such as the **New York City Draft Riots** of 1863, erupted throughout the country.

Antietam and Emancipation

The 1862 Union victory at the very bloody **Battle of Antietam** convinced Britain to abandon the struggling South and find new sources of cotton. Antietam also convinced Lincoln to fire the incompetent General **George McClellan**, commander of the Army of the Potomac, who was too battle-shy to engage the Confederacy's General **Robert E. Lee**. Lincoln also used the Antietam victory to issue his 1863 **Emancipation Proclamation**, which nominally freed all slaves in the secessionist South.

1863 and 1864

The **Battle of Gettysburg** and the **Battle of Vicksburg**, both in 1863, were the major turning points in the war: Union troops crushed Lee's forces at Gettysburg, while General **Ulysses S. Grant**'s victory at Vicksburg gave the Union control of the Mississippi and cracked the South in two.

In 1864, Grant also sent General **William Tecumseh Sherman** on his now-famous **March to the Sea** from Atlanta to Savannah, Georgia. Sherman's men destroyed everything in their path, including crops, homes, livestock, and the entire city of Atlanta. Sherman's rampage, along with the devastated economy, brought the South to its knees.

The Election of 1864

As the war dragged on into its fourth year, many Northerners began clamoring for peace. None were as loud as the **Peace Democrats**, or Copperheads, who wanted to negotiate a settlement with the South. They nominated George McClellan to run against Lincoln for the presidency in 1864. Lincoln and the Republicans, on the other hand, campaigned for continuation of the war until the South surrendered unconditionally and the Union was restored. Lincoln won, with 55 percent of the popular vote.

The Final Months

Lincoln's reelection spelled doom for the South. Unable to control his government, secure any outside help, or even feed his people, Davis requested peace negotiations as a final attempt to save the Confederacy. Lincoln, however, rejected his requests at the **Hampton Roads Conference** in February 1865, because Davis was unwilling to accept anything less than full independence. A month later, retreating Confederates burned Richmond to prevent Union troops from taking it before Grant cornered and defeated the remains of Lee's bedraggled army. Lee's unconditional surrender at Appomattox Courthouse on April 9, 1865, ended the war.

KEY PEOPLE & TERMS

PEOPLE

JOHN BROWN

A zealous, itinerant radical who crusaded violently against slavery in the 1850s. Brown moved to Kansas with his family in the mid-1850s to prevent the territory from becoming a slave state. In 1856, he and a band of vigilantes helped spark the **Bleeding Kansas** crisis when they slaughtered five **border ruffians** at the **Pottawatomie Massacre**. Three years later, Brown led another group of men in the **Harpers Ferry Raid** to incite a slave rebellion. He was captured during the raid and hanged shortly before the election of 1860. Brown's death was cheered in the South but mourned in the North.

JAMES BUCHANAN

A pro-Southern Democrat who became the fifteenth president of the United States in 1856. Buchanan defeated **John Frémont** of the new **Republican Party** and former president **Millard Fillmore** of the **Know-Nothing Party** in one of the most hotly contested elections in U.S. history. During his term, Buchanan supported the **Lecompton Constitution** to admit Kansas as a slave state, weathered the **Panic of 1857**, and did nothing to prevent South Carolina's secession from the Union.

JEFFERSON DAVIS

A former Senator from Mississippi who was selected as the first president of the Confederacy in 1861. Overworked and underappreciated by his fellow Confederates, Davis struggled throughout the Civil War to unify the Southern states under the central government they had established.

STEPHEN DOUGLAS

An influential Democratic senator and presidential candidate from Illinois. Douglas pushed the 1854 **Kansas-Nebraska Act** through Congress to entice railroad developers to build a transcontinental railroad line in the North. The act opened Kansas and Nebraska territories to slavery and thus effectively repealed the **Missouri Compromise** of 1820. A champion of **popular sovereignty**, he announced his **Freeport Doctrine** in the **Lincoln-Douglas** debates against **Abraham Lincoln** in 1858. Although Douglas was the most popular Democrat, Southern party members refused to nominate him for the presidency in 1860 because he had rejected the **Lecompton Constitution** to make Kansas a slave state. As a result, the party split: Northern Democrats nominated Douglas, while Southern Democrats nominated **John C. Breckinridge**. In the **election of 1860**, Douglas toured the country in an effort to save the Union.

ULYSSES S. GRANT
The Union's top general in the Civil War, who went on to become the eighteenth U.S. president. Nicknamed "Unconditional Surrender" Grant, he waged total war against the South in 1863 and 1864.

ROBERT E. LEE
Arguably the most brilliant general in the U.S. Army in 1860, who turned down **Abraham Lincoln**'s offer to command the Union forces in favor of commanding the Army of Northern Virginia for the Confederacy. Although Lee loved the United States, he felt he had to stand by his native state of Virginia. His defeat at the **Battle of Gettysburg** proved to be the turning point in the war in favor of the North. Lee made the Confederacy's unconditional **surrender at Appomattox Courthouse** to **Ulysses S. Grant** in April 1865 to end the Civil War.

ABRAHAM LINCOLN
A former lawyer from Illinois who became the sixteenth president of the United States in the election of 1860. Because Lincoln was a Republican and was associated with the abolitionist cause, his election prompted South Carolina to secede from the Union. Lincoln, who believed that the states had never truly left the Union legally, fought the war until the South surrendered unconditionally. During the war, in 1863, Lincoln issued the largely symbolic **Emancipation Proclamation** to free all slaves in the South. Just at the war's end, in April 1865, Lincoln was assassinated by John Wilkes Booth in Washington, D.C.

GEORGE MCCLELLAN
A young, first-rate U.S. Army general who commanded the Union army against the Confederates during the Civil War. Unfortunately, McClellan proved to be overly cautious and was always reluctant to engage Confederate forces at a time when **Abraham Lincoln** badly needed military victories to satisfy Northern public opinion. McClellan did manage to defeat **Robert E. Lee** at the **Battle of Antietam** in 1862, which gave Lincoln the opportunity to issue the **Emancipation Proclamation**. Lincoln eventually fired McClellan,

however, after the general began to criticize publicly the president's ability to command. In 1864, McClellan ran for president as a **Peace Democrat** on a platform for peace against Lincoln but was defeated.

FRANKLIN PIERCE
Fourteenth president of the United States, elected in 1852 as a pro-slavery Democrat from New England. Pierce combined his desire for empire and **westward expansion** with the South's desire to find new slave territories. He tacitly backed **William Walker**'s attempt to seize Nicaragua and used the **Ostend Manifesto** to try to acquire Cuba from Spain. Pierce also oversaw the opening of trade relations with Japan, upon the return of Commodore Matthew Perry, and authorized the **Gadsden Purchase** from Mexico in 1853.

WILLIAM TECUMSEH SHERMAN
A close friend of **Ulysses S. Grant** who served as a general in the Union army during the Civil War. Sherman, like Grant, understood that the war would only truly be won when the Union forces had broken the will of the Southern public to fight. Sherman is best known for the **total war** he and his expedition force waged on the South during his **March to the Sea**.

CHARLES SUMNER
A senator from Massachusetts who delivered an antislavery speech in the wake of the **Bleeding Kansas** crisis in 1856. In response, Sumner was caned nearly to death by South Carolinian congressman **Preston Brooks** on the Senate floor. The attack indicated just how passionately some Southerners viewed the popular sovereignty and slavery issue.

ZACHARY TAYLOR
A hero of the Mexican War who became the second and last **Whig** president in 1848. In order to avoid controversy over the westward expansion of slavery in the Mexican Cession, Taylor campaigned without a solid platform. He died after only sixteen months in office and was replaced by **Millard Fillmore**.

TERMS

BLEEDING KANSAS
A violent crisis that enveloped Kansas after Congress passed the **Kansas-Nebraska Act** in 1854. After the act passed, hundreds of Missourians crossed the border to make Kansas a slave state. Outraged

by the intimidation tactics these **"border ruffians"** used to bully settlers, many Northern abolitionists moved to Kansas as well in the
hopes of making the territory free. Tensions mounted until proslavery men burned the Free-Soil town of Lawrence, Kansas. **John
Brown** and a band of abolitionist vigilantes countered by killing five
men at the **Pottawatomie Massacre** in 1856. In many ways, Bleeding
Kansas was a prelude to the war that loomed ahead.

"BORDER RUFFIANS"

A group of hundreds of Missourians who crossed the border into
Kansas, hoping to make Kansas a slave state after Congress passed
the **Kansas-Nebraska Act** in 1854. The border ruffians rigged the
elections to choose delegates for the Kansas constitutional convention, with the aim of making Kansas a new slave state. They succeeded and drafted the proslavery **Lecompton Constitution** in the
winter of 1857. Outraged, many Northern abolitionists settled in
Kansas to counter the border ruffians. The territory erupted into a
civil war that became known as **Bleeding Kansas.** In 1858, the Senate
rejected the Lecompton Constitution on the grounds that the elections had been rigged.

COMPROMISE OF 1850

A bundle of legislation that enabled the North and South to end,
temporarily, the debate over the expansion of slavery. First proposed by **Henry Clay** and championed by **Stephen Douglas,** the Compromise of 1850 contained several provisions. California was
admitted as a free state; the other western territories were left to
popular sovereignty; the slave trade (but not slavery itself) was
banned in Washington, D.C.; Texas ceded disputed land to New
Mexico Territory; and a new **Fugitive Slave Law** was enacted.
Though the compromise was only a temporary solution, it effectively postponed the Civil War, and this extra time allowed the
Northern industrial economy to grow in the decade before the war.

DRED SCOTT V. SANFORD

A landmark 1857 Supreme Court decision that effectively ruled
that slaves were property. Dred Scott, a slave to a Southern army
doctor, had lived with his master in Illinois and Wisconsin in the
1830s. While there, he married a free woman and had a daughter.
Scott and his daughter eventually returned to the South. Scott sued his
master for his and his family's freedom, but Chief Justice **Roger Taney**
and a conservative Supreme Court ruled against Scott, arguing that

Congress had no right to restrict the movement of private property. Moreover, Taney ruled that blacks like Scott could not file lawsuits in federal courts because they were not citizens. The 1857 decision outraged Northerners and drove them further apart from the South.

EMANCIPATION PROCLAMATION

A presidential proclamation that nominally freed all slaves in the Confederacy. President **Abraham Lincoln**, emboldened by the Union victory at the **Battle of Antietam,** issued the proclamation on January 1, 1863. The proclamation did not free all slaves (North and South), because Lincoln did not want the proslavery **border states** to secede in anger. Though the proclamation had no immediate effect on black slaves in the South, it did mark an ideological turning point in the war, because it irrevocably linked emancipation with the restoration of the Union.

FREE-SOIL PARTY

A party formed by disgruntled Northern abolitionists in 1848, when Democrats nominated **Lewis Cass** for president and Whigs nominated the politically inept **Zachary Taylor.** Former president **Martin Van Buren** became the Free-Soil candidate for president, campaigning for the **Wilmot Proviso** and against **popular sovereignty** and the westward expansion of slavery. Van Buren received no votes in the electoral college but did detract enough popular votes from Cass to throw the election to Taylor.

FUGITIVE SLAVE ACT

A law passed under the **Compromise of 1850** that forced Northerners to return runaway slaves to the South. Angered by the fact that many Northerners supported the **Underground Railroad**, Southerners demanded this new and stronger Fugitive Slave Act as part of the compromise. The act was so unpopular in the North that federal troops were often required to enforce it. One slave in Boston, Massachusetts, had to be escorted by 300 soldiers and a U.S. Navy ship. The law, like the ***Dred Scott v. Sanford*** decision, drove the North and South even further apart.

HAMPTON ROADS CONFERENCE

A peace conference that **Jefferson Davis** requested in the winter of 1865, aware that the end of the war was near. At the conference, **Abraham Lincoln**'s representatives opened negotiations by demanding the unconditional surrender of the South and full emancipation of all slaves. The Southern delegation, however, refused anything less than full independence. The conference thus ended without resolution. However, the war ended only a few months later, completely on Lincoln's terms.

HARPERS FERRY RAID
An October 16, 1859, raid by **John Brown,** the infamous Free-Soiler who had killed five proslavery men at the **Pottawatomie Massacre.** This time around, Brown stormed an arsenal at Harpers Ferry, Virginia (present-day West Virginia), with twenty other men. He hoped the raid would prompt slaves throughout Virginia and the South to rise up against their masters. There was no rebellion, though, and Brown and his men found themselves cornered inside the arsenal. A long standoff ensued. Half the raiders were killed and the rest, including Brown, captured. After a speedy trial, Brown was convicted of treason and hanged. Although his death was cheered in the South, he became an abolitionist martyr in the North.

LECOMPTON CONSTITUTION
The Kansas constitution that resulted when hundreds of proslavery **border ruffians** from Missouri crossed into Kansas after the **Kansas-Nebraska Act** of 1854 and rigged the elections to choose delegates for the Kansas constitutional convention. The border ruffians succeeded and submitted the proslavery Lecompton Constitution in the winter of 1857. After taking office that same year, pro-Southern president **James Buchanan** immediately accepted the constitution to make Kansas a new slave state. Democrat **Stephen Douglas,** however, rejected the Lecompton Constitution in the Senate on the grounds that the elections had been rigged. The South denounced Douglas as a traitor when a new (and more honest) vote in Kansas overwhelmingly made the territory free. Kansas was admitted into the Union after the Civil War began.

LIBERTY PARTY
A Northern abolitionist party formed in 1840 when the abolitionist movement split into a social wing and a political wing. The Liberty Party nominated **James G. Birney** in the election of 1844 against Whig **Henry Clay** and Democrat **James K. Polk.** Surprisingly, the Liberty Party detracted just enough votes from Clay to throw the election to the Democrats.

LINCOLN-DOUGLAS DEBATES
A series of public debates between the relatively unknown former congressman **Abraham Lincoln** and **Stephen Douglas** in their home

state of Illinois in 1858. Hoping to steal Douglas's seat in the Senate in the national elections that year, Lincoln wanted to be the first to put the question of slavery to the voters. The "Little Giant" Douglas accepted and engaged Lincoln in a total of seven debates, each in front of several thousand people. Even though Lincoln lost the Senate seat, the debates made Lincoln a national figure.

PEACE DEMOCRATS

A Northern party, also nicknamed the "Copperheads" after the poisonous snake, that criticized **Abraham Lincoln** and the Civil War. The Peace Democrats did not particularly care that the Southern states had seceded and wanted to let them go in peace. The Copperheads nominated **George McClellan** for president in 1864 on a peace platform but lost to Lincoln and the Republican Party.

POPULAR SOVEREIGNTY

The idea that citizens in the West should vote to determine whether their respective territories would become free states or slave states upon admission to the Union. Popular sovereignty was first proposed by presidential candidate **Lewis Cass** in 1848 and later championed by **Stephen Douglas**. The **Whigs** and the **Republican Party** flatly rejected popular sovereignty, because they opposed the westward expansion of slavery.

POTTAWATOMIE MASSACRE

The killing of five proslavery men near Pottawatomie Creek, Kansas, by **John Brown** and a band of abolitionist vigilantes in retaliation for the burning of Free-Soil Lawrence, Kansas. Neither Brown nor any of his men were brought to justice. Instead, **border ruffians** and other proslavery settlers responded in kind and sparked the "**Bleeding Kansas**" crisis. Eventually, the entire territory became embroiled in a bloody civil war that foreshadowed the war between the North and South.

UNCLE TOM'S CABIN

A novel, published by **Harriet Beecher Stowe** in 1852, that turned Northern public opinion against slavery and the South more than anything else in the decade before the Civil War. *Uncle Tom's Cabin* became the first American bestseller almost overnight and went on to sell 250,000 copies in just a few short months. In the wake of the strengthened **Fugitive Slave Act**, Northerners identified with the black slave protagonist and pitied his suffering. The book affected the North so much that when **Abraham Lincoln** met Stowe in 1863, he called her "the little woman who wrote the book that made this great war."

Summary & Analysis

Expansion and Slavery: 1846–1855

Events

1846	Wilmot Proviso attempts to ban slavery in the West
1848	Mexican War ends Zachary Taylor elected president Free-Soil Party forms
1849	California and Utah request admittance to the Union
1850	Compromise of 1850 Congress passes Fugitive Slave Act Taylor dies; Millard Fillmore becomes president
1852	Harriet Beecher Stowe publishes *Uncle Tom's Cabin* Franklin Pierce elected president
1853	Gadsden Purchase negotiated
1854	Ostend Manifesto exposed
1855	William Walker invades Nicaragua

Key People

Zachary Taylor 12th U.S. president; avoided slavery issue; died sixteen months into term

Millard Fillmore 13th U.S. president; stepped in for deceased Taylor

Franklin Pierce 14th U.S. president; proslavery Democrat from New England; pursued expansionist policy in Latin America and the West

Lewis Cass Democratic presidential candidate in 1848; proposed popular sovereignty as means of determining free/slave status of western states

Henry Clay Kentucky statesman who engineered Compromise of 1850

Stephen Douglas Senator from Illinois; aided passage of the Compromise of 1850

Harriet Tubman Runaway slave from Maryland and active abolitionist; key figure in the Underground Railroad

The Wilmot Proviso

At the end of the **Mexican War**, many new lands west of Texas were yielded to the United States, and the debate over the westward expansion of slavery was rekindled. Southern politicians and slave owners demanded that slavery be allowed in the West because they feared that a closed door would spell doom for their economy and way of life. Whig Northerners, however, believed that slavery should be banned from the new territories. Pennsylvanian congressman David Wilmot proposed such a ban in 1846, even before the conclusion of the war. Southerners were outraged over this **Wilmot Proviso** and blocked it before it could reach the Senate.

SECTIONAL LOYALTY OVER PARTY LOYALTY

The Wilmot Proviso justified Southerners' fears that the North had designs against slavery. They worried that if politicians in the North prevented slavery from expanding westward, then it was only a matter of time before they began attacking it in the South as well. As a result, Southerners in both parties flatly rejected the proviso. Such bipartisan support was unprecedented and demonstrated just how serious the South really felt about the issue.

The large land concessions made to the U.S. in the 1848 **Treaty of Guadalupe Hidalgo** only exacerbated tensions. Debates in Congress grew so heated that fistfights even broke out between Northerners and Southerners on the floor of the House of Representatives. In fact, sectional division became so pronounced that many historians label the Mexican War and the Wilmot Proviso the first battles of the Civil War.

THE ELECTION OF 1848

Even though the Wilmot Proviso failed, the expansion of slavery remained the most pressing issue in the election of 1848. The Whigs nominated Mexican War hero General **Zachary Taylor,** a popular but politically inexperienced candidate who said nothing about the issue in hopes of avoiding controversy.

The Democrats, meanwhile, nominated **Lewis Cass.** Also hoping to sidestep the issue of slavery, Cass proposed allowing the citizens of each western territory to decide for themselves whether or not to be free or slave. Cass hoped that a platform based on such **popular sovereignty** would win him votes in both the North and South.

The election of 1848 also marked the birth of the **Free-Soil Party,** a hodgepodge collection of Northern abolitionists, former Liberty Party voters, and disgruntled Democrats and Whigs. The Free-Soilers nominated former president **Martin Van Buren,** who hoped to split the Democrats. He succeeded and diverted enough votes from Cass to throw the election in Taylor's favor. (Taylor, however, died after only sixteen months in office and was replaced by **Millard Fillmore.**)

THE SLAVERY DEBATE

Although Taylor's silence on the issue quieted the debate for about a year, the issue was revived when **California** and **Utah** applied for statehood. California's population had boomed after the 1849 **gold rush** had attracted thousands of prospectors, while barren Utah had blossomed due to the ingenuity of several thousand Mormons. The question arose whether these states should be admitted as free states or slave states. The future of slavery in Washington, D.C., was likewise in question.

A great debate ensued in Congress over the future of these three regions as Southerners attempted to defend their economic system while Northerners decried the evils of slavery. In Congress, the dying **John C. Calhoun** argued that the South still had every right to nullify unconstitutional laws and, if necessary, to secede from the Union it created. **Daniel Webster** and **Henry Clay**, on the other hand, championed the Union and compromise. Webster in particular pointed out that discussion over the expansion of slavery in the West was moot because western lands were unsuitable for growing cotton.

THE COMPROMISE OF 1850

In the end, the North and South agreed to compromise. Although Clay was instrumental in getting both sides to agree, he and Calhoun were too elderly and infirm to negotiate concessions and draft the necessary legislation. This task fell to a younger generation of politicians, especially the "Little Giant" **Stephen Douglas**, so named for his short stature and big mouth. A Democratic senator from Illinois, Douglas was responsible for pushing the finished piece of legislature through Congress.

The **Compromise of 1850**, as it was called, was a bundle of legislation that everyone could agree on. First, congressmen agreed that **California** would be admitted to the Union as a free state (Utah was not admitted because the Mormons refused to give up the practice of polygamy). The fate of slavery in the other territories, though, would be determined by **popular sovereignty**. Next, the slave trade (though not slavery itself) was banned in **Washington, D.C.** Additionally, **Texas** had to give up some of its land to form the New Mexican territory in exchange for a cancellation of debts owed to the federal government. Finally, Congress agreed to pass a newer and tougher **Fugitive Slave Act** to enforce the return of escaped slaves to the South.

A NORTHERN VICTORY IN 1850

Though both sides agreed to it, the Compromise of 1850 clearly favored the North over the South. California's admission as a free state not only set a precedent in the West against the expansion of slavery, but also ended the sectional balance in the Senate, with sixteen free states to fifteen slave states. Ever since the Missouri Compromise, this balance had always been considered essential to prevent the North from banning slavery. The South also conceded to end the slave trade in Washington, D.C., in exchange for debt

SUMMARY & ANALYSIS

relief for Texans and a tougher Fugitive Slave Law. Southerners were willing to make so many concessions because, like Northerners, they truly believed the Compromise of 1850 would end the debate over slavery. As it turned out, of course, they were wrong.

THE FUGITIVE SLAVE LAW

Ironically, the 1850 **Fugitive Slave Act** only fanned the abolitionist flame rather than put it out. Even though many white Americans in the North felt little love for blacks, they detested the idea of sending escaped slaves back to the South. In fact, armed mobs in the North freed captured slaves on several occasions, especially in New England, and violence against slave catchers increased despite the federal government's protests. On one occasion, it took several hundred troops and a naval ship to escort a single captured slave through the streets of Boston and back to the South. The Fugitive Slave Act thus allowed the abolitionists to transform their movement from a radical one to one that most Americans supported.

THE UNDERGROUND RAILROAD

Even though few slaves actually managed to escape to the North, the fact that Northern abolitionists encouraged slaves to run away infuriated Southern plantation owners. One network, the **Underground Railroad**, did successfully ferry as many as several thousand fugitive slaves into the North and Canada between 1840 and 1860. "Conductor" **Harriet Tubman**, an escaped slave from Maryland, personally delivered several hundred slaves to freedom.

UNCLE TOM'S CABIN

Another major boost for the abolitionist cause came via **Harriet Beecher Stowe**'s 1852 novel *Uncle Tom's Cabin*, a story about slavery in the South. Hundreds of thousands of copies were sold, awakening Northerners to the plight of enslaved blacks. The book affected the North so much that when Abraham Lincoln met Stowe in 1863, he commented, "So you're the little woman who wrote the book that made this great war!"

FRANKLIN PIERCE AND EXPANSION

Despite the concessions of the Compromise of 1850 and the growing abolitionist movement, Southerners believed the future of slavery to be secure, so they looked for new territories to expand the cotton kingdom. The election of **Franklin Pierce** in 1852 helped the Southern cause. A pro-South Democrat from New England, Pierce hoped to add more territory to the United States, in true Jacksonian fashion.

LATIN AMERICA AND THE OSTEND MANIFESTO

Pierce was particularly interested in acquiring new territories in Latin America and went as far as to quietly support **William Walker**'s takeover of Nicaragua. A proslavery Southerner, Walker hoped that Pierce would annex Nicaragua as Polk had annexed Texas in 1844. The plan failed, however, when several other Latin American countries sent troops to depose the adventurer. Pierce's reputation was also muddied over his threat to steal Cuba from Spain, which was revealed in a secret document called the **Ostend Manifesto**, which was leaked to the public in 1854.

THE GADSDEN PURCHASE

Despite his failures in Nicaragua and Cuba, Pierce did have several major successes during his term. In 1853, he completed negotiations to make the **Gadsden Purchase** from Mexico—30,000 square miles of territory in the southern portions of present-day Arizona and New Mexico. In addition, Pierce successfully opened Japan to American trade that same year.

BLEEDING KANSAS: 1854–1856

EVENTS

1854	Congress passes Kansas-Nebraska Act
	Republican Party forms
1856	Border ruffians burn the town of Lawrence, Kansas
	Pottawatomie Massacre
	Charles Sumner attacked in the Senate
	James Buchanan elected president

KEY PEOPLE

John Brown Violent radical abolitionist involved in the Pottawatomie Massacre and Harpers Ferry Raid

James Buchanan 15th U.S. president; pro-Southern Democrat

Stephen Douglas Democratic senator from Illinois; pushed the Kansas-Nebraska Act through Congress

John Frémont Mexican War hero; first presidential candidate for the new Republican Party

SUMMARY & ANALYSIS

THE KANSAS-NEBRASKA ACT

Senator **Stephen Douglas** of Illinois, hoping to lure transcontinental railroad developers away from lands acquired via the **Gadsden Purchase**, proposed instead to build the line farther north, so that the railway would end in Chicago and give his home region a huge economic boost. But federal law required that the vast unorganized areas in the middle of the country first be carved into official territories before any track could be laid.

To do so, Douglas rammed the **Kansas-Nebraska Act** through Congress in 1854 to create two new territories—Kansas in the South and Nebraska in the North. According to the **Missouri Compromise** of 1820, both territories would have to be free because they were north of the 36° 30' line. But Douglas, aware that Southern legislatures would never approve two new free territories, declared instead that **popular sovereignty** would determine whether Kansas and Nebraska would be free or slave. In doing so, he hoped to strengthen his bid for the presidency in 1856 by winning support from Southern Democrats.

BACKLASH AGAINST THE KANSAS-NEBRASKA ACT

Because popular sovereignty had worked in the Compromise of 1850, Douglas assumed that the doctrine would work in the unorganized territories as well. Privately, he believed that slavery would never take hold in Kansas and Nebraska because the terrain was unsuitable for producing cotton. Popular sovereignty, then, was merely a carrot to appease the South. Douglas thus figured the act would please both the abolitionists in the North and slave owners in the South, bring development to Chicago, and increase his chances for the party's nomination in 1856 without really changing anything.

But Douglas's plan backfired. Southerners—Democrats and Whigs alike—jumped at the opportunity to open Northern territories to slavery, but Northerners recoiled, outraged that the Missouri Compromise had been violated. Riots and protests against the Kansas-Nebraska Act erupted in Northern cities.

GROWING ANTISLAVERY SENTIMENTS IN THE NORTH

What Douglas had failed to realize was that most Northerners regarded the Missouri Compromise to be almost sacred. The publication of *Uncle Tom's Cabin* and the brutal enforcement of the **Fugitive Slave Act** had by this time awakened hundreds of thousands in the North to the horrors of slavery. Even those who benefited from Southern slavery, such as textile manufacturers, did not wish to see slavery expand further west or north. The Kansas-Nebraska Act succeeded only in shifting Northern public opinion even further away from reconciliation with the South.

THE END OF THE WHIG PARTY

The Kansas-Nebraska Act also caused the collapse of both the Whig and Democratic parties. The parties split according to section: to pass the act through Congress, Southern Whigs voted with Southern Democrats against their Northern counterparts for the first time in history. The Whigs were never able to reunite after this catastrophic divide. The Democrats survived, but Northern Democrats lost over half their seats in Congress that year.

BORDER RUFFIANS VS. FREE-SOILERS

After the Kansas-Nebraska Act, thousands of people moved into the territory. Most of them were simply westward-moving farmers in search of better land, but others swarmed there in an attempt to tip the balance in the impending decision about Kansas's free/slave status. Thousands of proslavery Missourians crossed the state line into Kansas when they learned that popular sovereignty would determine the fate of slavery. They grabbed as much land as they could and established dozens of small towns. These **"border ruffians"** also rigged unfair elections, sometimes recruiting friends and family in Missouri to cross over into Kansas and cast illegal ballots. Others voted multiple times or threatened honest locals to vote for slavery. Afraid that Kansas would become the next slave state, Northern abolitionists flocked there too and established their own **Free-Soil towns**. Both factions even went so far as to establish their own territorial capitals.

"BLEEDING KANSAS"

Inevitably, the two groups clashed. In one incident, a hotheaded band of proslavery settlers burned the Free-Soil town of Lawrence, Kansas. In retaliation, the deranged **John Brown** and his own antislavery band killed five border ruffians in the **Pottawatomie Massacre**. Neither Brown nor any of his followers were ever tried for their crimes. Within a few months, Kansas was plagued by marauding violent factions. This rampant lawlessness and bloodshed earned the territory the nickname "**Bleeding Kansas**."

CHARLES SUMNER

Blood was also spilled over Kansas on the Senate floor when Congressman **Preston Brooks** of South Carolina beat Massachusetts Senator **Charles Sumner** brutally with his cane. Brooks had grown so incensed over the antislavery speech Sumner had delivered the previous week that he decided to take vengeance on his own. The beating nearly killed Sumner, who was forced to leave the Senate for several years to receive medical treatment. Brooks was hailed as a hero in the South but vilified in the North.

THE ELECTION OF 1856

Americans were still divided over the Kansas issue as the **election of 1856** approached, so parties nominated Kansas-neutral candidates in the hopes of overcoming the growing sectionalism. The Whig Party had by this time dissolved into Northern and Southern factions and was unable to agree on a candidate. Northern Whigs instead united with **Free-Soil Party** members and Unionist Democrats to form the new **Republican Party** and nominate adventurer **John C. Frémont**. Democrats, on the other hand, rallied behind the relatively unknown **James Buchanan**. Whereas Frémont ran on a platform expressly opposed to the westward expansion of slavery, Buchanan campaigned for popular sovereignty. The nativist **Know-Nothing Party** also entered ex-president **Millard Fillmore** in the race, campaigning on a platform to stem the influx of Irish and German immigrants. In the end, Buchanan defeated his rivals soundly.

THE BUCHANAN YEARS: 1857–1858

EVENTS

1857	Buchanan accepts Lecompton Constitution
	Supreme Court issues *Dred Scott v. Sanford* decision
	Panic of 1857
1858	Congress rejects Lecompton Constitution
	Lincoln and Douglas debate slavery in Illinois

KEY PEOPLE

James Buchanan 15th U.S. president; supported the Lecompton Constitution to admit Kansas as a slave state

Dred Scott Slave who sued his master for his and his family's freedom in a landmark 1857 Supreme Court case

Roger Taney Chief Justice of the Supreme Court who declared the Missouri Compromise unconstitutional in the *Dred Scott v. Sanford* decision

Stephen Douglas Illinois senator who rejected Kansas's Lecompton Constitution; announced Freeport Doctrine of popular sovereignty during the Lincoln-Douglas debates in 1858

Abraham Lincoln Former lawyer from Illinois who rose to national prominence during the Lincoln-Douglas debates

DRED SCOTT V. SANFORD

Just two days after **James Buchanan** became president in 1857, controversy over the slavery issue struck again when the Supreme Court declared the Missouri Compromise unconstitutional in the ***Dred Scott v. Sanford*** case. In the infamous decision, the enslaved **Dred Scott** sued his master for his freedom and that of his wife and daughter. Scott had married a free black woman while traveling with his master in the free state of Illinois in the 1830s. The two had a child but then moved back to the South. Scott believed that he had been freed once he had crossed the 36° 30' parallel and that his wife and daughter had been enslaved illegally when they returned to the South.

However, Chief Justice **Roger Taney**, along with a majority of the other justices—all but one from the South—ruled that the Missouri Compromise was unconstitutional because the federal government had no right to restrict the movement of property (i.e., slaves). Taney also contended that Scott had no business suing his master in a U.S. court, because that right was reserved only for citizens. Taney hoped his ruling would finalize blacks' status as property, uphold slavery, and end the divisive sectional debates.

NORTHERN BACKLASH

The *Dred Scott* ruling only exacerbated sectional tensions, however. Whereas Southerners hailed it as a landmark decision that would finally bring peace, Northerners were appalled. Thousands in the North took to the streets to protest the decision, and many questioned the impartiality of the Southern-dominated Supreme Court. Several state legislatures essentially nullified the decision and declared that they would never permit slavery within their borders, no matter who ordered them to do so. Buchanan himself was implicated when it was discovered that he had pressured the Northern justice into voting with the Southerners. Arguably, the *Dred Scott* decision had almost as great an effect on Northern public opinion as *Uncle Tom's Cabin.*

THE LECOMPTON CONSTITUTION

Meanwhile, the bleeding had not stopped in Kansas, where **abolitionist settlers** and **border ruffians**, unable to agree on a territorial government, established two separate ones—a Free-Soil legislature in Topeka and a proslavery legislature in Lecompton. After the Free-Soilers boycotted a rigged election to draft a state constitution in 1857, proslavery settlers were given a free hand to write the document as they sought fit. When they finished this **Lecompton Constitution,** they then applied for statehood as a slave state.

President Buchanan accepted the constitution immediately and welcomed Kansas into the Union. In 1858, however, the Republican-dominated Congress refused to admit Kansas on the grounds that border ruffians had rigged the election. **Stephen Douglas** declared that Kansas would be admitted only after honest elections were held to determine whether the state would be free or slave. The Lecompton Constitution was put to a special vote in the territory the following year and was soundly defeated. Kansas eventually entered the Union as a free state in 1861.

THE PANIC OF 1857

Buchanan's other major challenge was the brief economic depression that swept the nation in 1857 and 1858. The depression was sparked by the **Panic of 1857**, which occurred when newspapers reported the failure of a prominent bank in the Midwest. Reduced exports of food and manufactured goods made the depression worse in the West and North but left the South's cotton economy relatively untouched. Southerners relished Britain's dependence on cotton and hailed the soaring unemployment rate in the North as proof that the **wage-labor system** had failed.

THE LINCOLN-DOUGLAS DEBATES

In this atmosphere of national confusion, relatively unknown former congressman **Abraham Lincoln** challenged **Stephen Douglas** to a series of public debates in their home state of Illinois. Lincoln, hoping to steal Douglas's seat in the Senate in the 1858 elections, wanted to be the first to put the question of slavery to the voters. The "Little Giant" accepted and engaged Lincoln in a total of seven debates, each in front of several thousand people.

During the debates, Lincoln denounced slavery as a moral wrong and argued that the "peculiar institution" should be banned from the West permanently. At the same time, though, he also called for the preservation of the Union. Douglas accused Lincoln of being a radical abolitionist and articulated a new policy—the **Freeport Doctrine**—stating that popular sovereignty in the territories was the only democratic solution to resolving the slavery problem. Even though Lincoln lost the Senate race, the **Lincoln-Douglas debates** brought him to national prominence.

SUMMARY & ANALYSIS

THE ELECTION OF 1860 AND SECESSION: 1859–1861

EVENTS

1859	John Brown raids Harpers Ferry, Virginia
1860	Abraham Lincoln elected president South Carolina secedes from the Union
1861	Alabama, Florida, Georgia, Louisiana, Mississippi, and Texas secede Jefferson Davis becomes president of the Confederate States of America Lincoln delivers first inaugural address South Carolina seizes Fort Sumter Arkansas, North Carolina, Tennessee, and Virginia secede

KEY PEOPLE

Abraham Lincoln 16th U.S. president; his Republican roots and association with abolitionism prompted South Carolina to secede in 1861

John Bell Constitutional Union candidate for president in 1860; campaigned for compromise, Union, and slavery

John C. Breckinridge Vice president under Buchanan and Democratic candidate for president in 1860; supported by Southern Democrats

Stephen Douglas Democratic presidential candidate in 1860; supported primarily by Northern Democrats

Jefferson Davis Former senator from Mississippi selected as president of the Confederate States of America in 1861

William Seward Radical abolitionist who led Whig Party and, later, Republican Party

John Brown Radical abolitionist who incited a slave uprising in Harpers Ferry, Virginia, in 1859; was convicted of treason and hanged

JOHN BROWN AND HARPERS FERRY

Although the economic depression of 1857–1858 put a temporary damper on the slavery debate, the radical abolitionist **John Brown** quickly revived it with another violent incident. On October 16, 1859, Brown—the infamous Free-Soiler who had killed five proslavery men at the **Pottawatomie Massacre** in Kansas in 1856—stormed an arsenal at **Harpers Ferry**, Virginia (present-day West Virginia), with twenty other men. He hoped the raid would prompt slaves throughout Virginia and the South to rise up against their masters.

Strangely, though, the fanatical Brown had never informed the slaves of his plan, so no uprising took place, and Brown and his men found themselves cornered inside the arsenal. A long standoff ended with half the raiders dead and the rest, including Brown, captured. After a speedy trial, Brown was convicted of treason and hanged. Before his death, he announced that he would gladly die if his death brought the nation closer to justice.

Brown's execution was met with cheers in the South and wails in the North. His raid had touched on Southerners' deepest fear that their slaves would one day rise up against them, and many in the South viewed him as a criminal and a traitor of the worst kind. Most Northerners, however, saw Brown as a martyr, especially after he so boldly denounced slavery with his final words.

DEMOCRATIC CANDIDATES IN 1860

Amid this tense atmosphere, the nation's political parties convened to select their respective candidates for the presidential election of 1860. Democrats gathered in Charleston, South Carolina, but were bitterly deadlocked on whom to nominate. Though **Stephen Douglas** was the party favorite, no Southern Democrat would vote for him after he had rejected the **Lecompton Constitution** in 1858. Unable to compromise, the party split: Northern Democrats returned home and nominated Douglas, while Southern Democrats chose proslavery Vice President **John C. Breckinridge** from Kentucky.

REPUBLICAN CANDIDATES IN 1860

The Republicans also had trouble choosing a candidate. Senator **William Seward** from New York was the most popular choice but also the riskiest because of his hard-line antislavery stance. Moreover, the Republicans knew they needed a candidate who could win both the Northeast and the contested Northwest (now called the Midwest), where the Democrats had a strong foothold.

As a result, the Republicans settled on the lanky **Abraham Lincoln** from Illinois, who had a reputation in the North for being a moderate and a Unionist. Nonetheless, a small faction of Republicans saw Lincoln as too much of an abolitionist and instead nominated Tennessean **John Bell** under the banner of the proslavery **Constitutional Union Party**.

THE ELECTION OF 1860

With the parties split and compromise no longer a solution, the **election of 1860** was less a national election that two sectional elections. Most Southern states refused to put Lincoln's name on the ballot or acknowledge his candidacy, and several even vowed to leave the Union if Lincoln were elected. Few people took this secession talk seriously, however, for the South had been making similar threats for decades.

The run-up to the election was intense as the four major candidates crisscrossed the country discussing the issues. On top of their traditional platform of higher tariffs and internal improvements, Lincoln and the Republicans added the promise of maintaining the Union.

The Constitutional Union candidate, Bell, likewise promised to preserve the Union. Northern Democrat Douglas delivered antisecession speeches, and Southern Democrat Breckinridge defended slavery.

In the end, Lincoln won a resounding victory, with 40 percent of the popular vote. He won a total of 180 electoral votes, while the other candidates combined won 123.

SECESSION

A month after Lincoln's election, legislators in **South Carolina** voted unanimously to secede; within several weeks, **Alabama**, **Florida**, **Georgia**, **Louisiana**, **Mississippi**, and **Texas** followed suit. Despite "Honest Abe's" reputation in the North as a moderate, he was vilified as a radical abolitionist "Black Republican" in the South. Much to the dismay of anxious Northerners, lame-duck president **James Buchanan** did nothing to address the secession crisis. Lincoln also waited to take action until he had officially become president.

THE CONFEDERATE STATES OF AMERICA

Meanwhile, delegates from the seven secessionist states met in Montgomery, Alabama, in February 1861 to form the government of the new **Confederate States of America**. They drafted a new constitution; chose **Richmond**, Virginia, to be the new capital; and selected former Mississippi senator **Jefferson Davis** as the Confederacy's first president. (*For more information about the Confederate government, see* The Confederate Side, *p. 34.*)

THE CRITTENDEN COMPROMISE

Hoping to prevent war from breaking out after the secession, Senator **John Crittenden** from Kentucky proposed another compromise. He suggested adding an **amendment** to the Constitution to protect slavery in all territories south of 36° 30', and then allowing **popular sovereignty** to determine whether these Southern territories became free or slave when they applied for statehood. All territories north of 36° 30', meanwhile, would be free. Many Southerners contemplated the **Crittenden Compromise**, but Lincoln rejected it on the grounds that he had been elected to block the westward expansion of slavery.

LINCOLN'S FIRST INAUGURAL ADDRESS

As both Northerners and Southerners waited to see how Lincoln would respond, he calmly announced in his **first inaugural address** that he would do nothing. Rather, he reaffirmed the North's friendship with the South, stressed national unity, and asked Southerners to abandon secession. Moreover, he declared that the secession was illegal and that he would maintain the Union at all costs—but that he would make no move against the South unless provoked.

In announcing that he himself would take no action, Lincoln placed the responsibility for any future violence squarely on the South's shoulders. He knew that Americans in the North would support a war only in which the Southerners were the aggressors. Lincoln could thus continue to claim honestly that he was fighting to defend and save the Union from those who wished to tear it apart.

FORT SUMTER

Jefferson Davis, on the other hand, announced in his inaugural speech that the South might be required to use force to secure its aims, and that spring, the South made good on its word. On April 12, 1861, General **P. T. Beauregard** ordered his South Carolinian militia unit to attack **Fort Sumter**, a Union stronghold on an island in Charleston Harbor. After a day of intense bombardment, Major Robert Anderson surrendered the fort to Beauregard. South Carolina's easy victory prompted four more states—**Arkansas**, **North Carolina**, **Tennessee**, and **Virginia**—to secede. The Civil War had begun.

COMPLACENCY IN THE SOUTH

The fall of Fort Sumter was not a major battle, militarily speaking: the Union troops surrendered only because they ran out of supplies, and neither side suffered any serious casualties. However, the easy seizure of Fort Sumter inspired complacency in the South: Southerners misinterpreted Anderson's surrender as a sign that the Union was weak and unwilling to fight.

Lincoln's lack of immediate response was likewise misleading. The North appeared to do nothing for months afterward—the next battle wasn't fought until July—and the South interpreted this inaction as further weakness. In reality, Lincoln used the interim weeks to ready the military and put the gears of the North's war machine into motion. The brutal war that followed turned out to be far different from the smooth sailing the South initially expected.

THE UNION SIDE: 1861–1863

EVENTS

1861	Congress passes Morrill Tariff
	Lincoln suspends writ of habeas corpus
	Trent Affair occurs
1862	Congress passes Legal Tender Act, Homestead Act, and Morrill Land Grant Act
1863	Congress passes National Banking Act
	Drafts initiated in the North
	Draft riots in New York City
	France invades Mexico

KEY PEOPLE

Abraham Lincoln 16th U.S. president; tested limits of constitutional powers with several
    controversial executive orders during the war

THE BORDER STATES

When South Carolina seceded from the Union in 1860, only ten of
the other fourteen slave states followed. The legislatures of the
remaining four—**Maryland, Delaware, Kentucky,** and **Missouri**—
chose to remain in the Union. **West Virginia** eventually seceded from
Virginia in 1861 and then in 1863 was admitted as a nonslave state
in the Union.

To ensure the continued loyalty of these **border states,** Lincoln
always had to maintain a moderate course in his policies. At times,
he had to resort to force to prevent the border states from joining the
Confederacy. In the spring of 1861, for example, Lincoln declared
martial law in Maryland and sent troops to occupy the state after
protesters attacked Union soldiers marching to Washington, D.C.

IMPORTANCE OF THE BORDER STATES

Had the border states seceded with the other slave states, the outcome of the Civil War might have been very different. First, the border states provided a geographical and ideological buffer between
the combatants: had Maryland seceded, Washington, D.C., would
have been entirely surrounded by Confederate territory. Second, the
border states were important economic engines for the Union, primarily because Maryland and Delaware had so many factories. Had
just those two states seceded, the Confederacy's manufacturing
capabilities would have nearly doubled. Because the Civil War was
in many ways an economic war as much as a military one, doubling
Southern manufacturing output could have seriously altered the
duration and even the outcome of the war.

The fact that these slave states chose to remain in the Union also weakened the South's claim that it had seceded to save its slavery-based economy. Nevertheless, Lincoln had to be careful not to offend slave owners in the border states, which is why, for example, the 1863 Emancipation Proclamation declared slaves free in only the secessionist states—not the loyal border states.

CONTROVERSIAL WARTIME ACTS

During the war, Lincoln faced opposition and criticism from a variety of groups in the North. **Peace Democrats** accused him of starting an unjust war on one side, while **Radical Republicans** in his own party accused him of being too soft on the Confederacy on the other.

In addition, many criticized Lincoln for using **unconstitutional powers** to achieve his goals. To prevent an insurrection in Maryland, he arrested several proslavery leaders in the state, suspended the writ of **habeas corpus** (which requires police to inform suspects of the charges against them), and imprisoned them until the war was over. Chief Justice of the Supreme Court **Roger Taney** ruled that the suspension was illegal and unconstitutional, but Lincoln ignored him, believing that his actions had been necessary to prevent further rebellion.

Lincoln also illegally ordered a **naval blockade** of the South (which only Congress could do), illegally increased the **size of the army** (again, a power reserved only for Congress), and authorized **illegal voting methods** in the border states. Congress generally supported all of these decisions. Lincoln justified them by claiming that desperate times called for desperate measures and promised to obey the Constitution once the war was over.

THE MORRILL TARIFF

The 1862 Congress, for its part, passed a flurry of progressive new laws as soon as the South had seceded from the Union. First, Northern congressmen passed the protective **Morrill Tariff**, which essentially doubled the prewar tariff. They passed the tariff not only to win more support from manufacturers but also because they realized how important the economy would be during the war.

THE LEGAL TENDER ACT AND NATIONAL BANK ACT

Next, Congress passed the 1862 **Legal Tender Act**, which authorized the printing of a national currency of paper money that was not redeemable for gold or silver. The next year, the **National Bank Act** provided for the federal charter of banks and supervision of a system of national banks, all of which were required to comply with the Legal Tender Act.

The Homestead Act

Congress also passed the **Homestead Act**, which gave individual settlers 160 acres of western land if they promised to live on the land and improve it by farming and building a house. In addition, Congress passed the **Morrill Land Grant Act**, which provided federal lands to state governments to build new agricultural colleges.

Congress Without Southerners

As one historian put it, Congress was so productive in 1861, 1862, and 1863 precisely because there were no conservative Southerners to oppose new legislation. Without any states' righters, Northern Republicans could pass higher tariffs, write a wide variety of badly needed reform bills, strengthen the national economy, and bolster the federal government.

The new laws eliminated countless different currencies in circulation that had been issued by individual states or banks and replaced them with a single dollar backed by gold in the U.S. Treasury. The new **greenback** dollar (named for its color) gave the North great economic stability, which eventually helped it beat the South. Together, the acts gave the federal government unprecedented power over the economy. The Morrill Land Grant Act and the Homestead Act, meanwhile boosted settlement and the agricultural development of the West during the war and for several decades afterward.

The Draft and Draft Riots

In 1863, Congress passed a **conscription law** to draft young men into the Union army. The law demanded that men either join the army or make a $300 contribution to the war effort instead. The "$300 rule" thus effectively condemned the poorer classes to military service while giving wealthier men a way out. Outraged, many Northerners engaged in massive protests, and **draft riots** broke out in dozens of cities throughout the North. The worst erupted in New York City in mid-1863, when whites from poorer neighborhoods burned and looted parts of the city. By the time federal troops arrived to suppress the rebellion, more than 100 people had been killed.

The Trent Affair

Surprisingly, Lincoln spent a great deal of effort trying to preserve diplomatic ties with **Britain** during the war. Soon after the war began, Union naval officers boarded the British mail ship *Trent* in 1861 in order to arrest two Confederate diplomats. The **Trent Affair** outraged Britain, which threatened Lincoln with war if he failed to

THE CIVIL WAR ❦ 33

release the Southerners. The situation became so serious that thousands of British troops were dispatched to Canada to prepare for a possible invasion. Lincoln eventually apologized and let the Confederates go.

The United States, in turn, later threatened war if Britain refused to stop building warships—such as the **CSS *Alabama***—for the Confederacy. This time, Britain conceded. War between Britain and the U.S. almost broke out a third time in 1864, when Canada harbored Confederate fugitives. Britain sent more troops to Canada to prepare for war, but an agreement was reached before any shots were fired.

THE NORTHERN ECONOMY

Ultimately, it was the North's booming **industrial economy**—assisted by the Morrill Tariff, the Legal Tender Act, and the National Bank Act—that won the Civil War. When war broke out in 1861, almost all of the nation's factories were located in the North. Manufacturers also increased production of **agricultural equipment** to help the farmers in the West produce more wheat and corn to feed the troops. **Oil production** and **coal mining** became big industries during these years as well.

Because the Confederacy had virtually no textile factories, Confederate troops often fought in tattered homespun uniforms. The South also had precious few rifle factories, so its troops were forced to fight with pistols, smuggled guns, and even old Revolutionary War muskets instead of the newer and more efficient rifles that Union soldiers used. Furthermore, the South had the misfortune of suffering severe droughts several summers during the war, so its troops were not as well fed as the Northern forces

THE CONFEDERATE SIDE: 1861–1863

EVENTS

1861	Jefferson Davis becomes president of the Confederate States of America
1862	Confederacy passes Conscription Act
	U.S. Congress passes Confiscation Act
1863	Bread riots in Richmond, Virginia

KEY PEOPLE

Jefferson Davis President of the Confederacy; struggled throughout the war to unify the Southern states under their central government

INITIAL JUBILATION

A feeling of triumph erupted throughout the South when the Confederate government was formed in 1861. A sense of liberation pervaded the secessionist states, as Southerners believed they could finally be free from the tyrannous North, which sought to undermine the slave-based economy and Southern way of life. Most secessionists saw themselves as neopatriots, carrying on the revolutionary tradition of their forefathers to safeguard liberty. Many in the South saw Lincoln as the new King George III of Britain and viewed the South as the righteous underdog.

Southerners were also optimistic about their chances of winning the war. They realized that the North would have to fight an offensive war on Southern territory, whereas the South had only to fight a **limited war** to defeat Union armies or match them in a stalemate. As a result, many Southerners saw victory as inevitable.

THE CONFEDERATE GOVERNMENT

Delegates from the first seven states to secede—South Carolina, Mississippi, Alabama, Georgia, Florida, Texas, and Louisiana—formed the government of the new **Confederate States of America** in Montgomery, Alabama, in February 1861. They wrote a new constitution, established a new capital at Richmond, and chose **Jefferson Davis** as president.

FEDERATION VS. CONFEDERATION

Although the government of the Confederacy looked on the surface much like the government of the United States—the Confederacy used the U.S. Constitution as a template—the two were in reality quite different. As states' righters, the drafters of the Confederate constitution made sure that their federal government was relatively weaker than the governments of the individual states. Whereas the

United States was a **federation** of states bound by a strong central government, the South was a decentralized **confederation** of states loosely allied with each other for common defense. In many ways, the Confederacy resembled the United States under the **Articles of Confederation**. As it turned out, though, the Confederacy's weak central government proved to be a major handicap during the war.

JEFFERSON DAVIS
Although Davis had had more political experience than Lincoln—he had served as secretary of war and as a U.S. senator—he proved an ineffective commander-in-chief. Unlike Lincoln, he underestimated the importance of public opinion and as a result did not connect well with voters. Moreover, his nervousness and refusal to delegate authority alienated many of his cabinet secretaries, cabinet members, and state governors. As a result, he often had difficulty controlling his government.

CONFEDERATE DISUNITY
The Confederacy's greatest weakness was the difficulty Davis's government had in controlling the individual states—the same problem the national Congress had faced under the Articles of Confederation. Though Davis attempted to assemble a **national army** to match the powerful Union forces, the Southern states did not work together to facilitate the undertaking, and Davis had no real way to force the state governors to comply and send men. As the war dragged on, some governors even refused to let their troops cross state lines to assist fellow Confederates who needed backup.

Also like the national Congress under the Articles, the Confederate government had serious financial troubles throughout the war because few states paid their fair share. The central government even had trouble keeping the Confederacy together during the war: in 1861, Unionists in western regions of Virginia seceded from the Confederacy and then rejoined the Union as the new state of **West Virginia** two years later.

THE CONSCRIPTION ACT
The Richmond government did manage to pass the **Conscription Act** of 1862 to draft young men in all the Confederate states into the national army. As Richmond got more desperate for troops, the draft was extended to middle-aged men as well. The law, like the North's law, was biased against poorer Southerners in favor of the elite. Wealthy planters and landowners were exempt from the draft,

as were overseers and anyone else whose job was vital to maintaining control over the slaves. As a result, the army was filled with farmers and landless whites, many of them disgruntled. Blacks were excluded from military service.

CONFEDERATE DIPLOMACY

One of the Confederacy's most pressing goals during the war was to secure **international recognition from Europe** and enter a **military alliance with Britain**. International recognition would legitimize the Confederacy and justify its cause. An alliance with Britain would break the Union blockade of Southern ports and supply the Confederacy with arms and badly needed manufactured goods.

BRITISH ASSISTANCE

At the war's outset, Confederate policymakers banked on recognition and an alliance because they believed Britain was very dependent on Southern **cotton**. Planters in the Confederacy provided 75 percent of the cotton that British textile manufacturers consumed.

Indeed, Britain allowed Southern ships to use its ports and even built Confederate warships, such as the *Alabama*, which sank more than sixty Union ships on the high seas. British shipbuilders also agreed to build two ironclad warships with **Laird rams**, which the Confederates could use to pierce the hulls of enemy ships.

BRITISH DETACHMENT

Unfortunately for the South, however, Davis was never able to parlay this British assistance into a formal recognition or alliance. First, the Confederate government had overestimated Britain's cotton dependence. Although most of Britain's cotton came from the South, it became clear that British textile manufacturers had bought from the South only because it was cheaper. As a result, though the **Union blockade** of Southern ports temporarily hurt the British textile industry, the industry bounced back quickly after switching to cotton suppliers from Egypt and India.

Perhaps more important, despite London's rocky relationship with Washington, D.C., war threats from Lincoln kept the British at bay, especially after the resounding Union victory at the Battle of Antietam (*see* Major Battles, *p. 38*). As a result, the Laird rams were eventually scrapped, and Richmond lost all hope for help from the outside.

COLLAPSE OF THE SOUTHERN ECONOMY

Unable to break through the Union blockade—and thus unable to buy goods or sell cotton—the Confederacy experienced a massive

economic collapse in 1862 and never recovered. Individual states and private banks printed more cheap paper money to counter the depression, but these measures only worsened the situation by causing **inflation**.

This inflation spiraled into a situation of **hyperinflation**, in which the value of the Confederate dollar dropped rapidly, sometimes even from hour to hour. Meanwhile, because of drought conditions, food became scarce in some areas. In 1863, things got so bad that a group of Virginians, many of them women, looted the Confederate capital in the **Richmond Bread Riots**, searching for food and taking out their frustration on their government.

SUMMARY & ANALYSIS

MAJOR BATTLES: 1861–1863

EVENTS

1861	South Carolina attacks Fort Sumter
	Confederacy defeats Union at First Battle of Bull Run
1862	Union defeats Confederacy at Shiloh and Antietam
1863	Lincoln issues Emancipation Proclamation
	Union defeats Confederacy at Gettysburg and Vicksburg
	Lincoln delivers Gettysburg Address

KEY PEOPLE

Abraham Lincoln 16th U.S. president; ordered Union naval blockade of the South; delivered landmark Gettysburg Address

Robert E. Lee General who turned down Lincoln's offer to command Union forces in favor of commanding the Army of Northern Virginia for the Confederacy

George McClellan Young general who commanded the Union's Army of the Potomac but was later fired after criticizing Lincoln publicly and failing to engage Lee's forces

Ulysses S. Grant Top Union general after McClellan's termination; waged total war against the South starting in 1863, including major victory at Vicksburg

PREPARING FOR WAR

After the seizure of **Fort Sumter** in April 1861, both the North and the South prepared for war. The North had a distinct **economic advantage** because almost all of the nation's factories were been located in the Northeast and Mid-Atlantic states. The Union also had nearly twice the South's **population** and thus a larger pool of young men to serve in the army.

LACK OF LEADERSHIP IN THE NORTH

However, the North's new recruits were largely untrained, and most of the best military commanders had been from the South. **Abraham Lincoln** offered command of the main Union army to **Robert E. Lee**, but Lee, though he disapproved of secession, felt compelled to fight for his home state of Virginia.

GEORGE MCCLELLAN

Lincoln therefore ended up putting General **George McClellan** in command of the **Army of the Potomac**. "Little Mac," as he was called, though still only in his thirties, was probably the most popular man in the army in his day. Despite McClellan's popularity with the troops, however, he was poorly regarded among civilian leaders in Washington and had a reputation for having a rather large ego. Throughout the war, McClellan proved timid, and he always made some excuse to avoid engaging Lee's **Army of Northern Virginia.**

THE FIRST BATTLE OF BULL RUN

War preparations took some time, so it was not until three months after Fort Sumter that Union and Confederate troops met again at the **First Battle of Bull Run** in Virginia, between Washington, D.C., and Richmond. Still believing that the war was a trifling matter that would be over quickly, a number of government officials and spectators from both sides came to "observe" the battle, some even packing picnic lunches. By the end of the day, Union forces had lost and were forced to retreat. The loss shocked Northerners out of their complacency and prompted them to prepare more seriously for the struggle ahead. Meanwhile, many Southerners interpreted the victory as an indicator of an early end to the war and as decisive proof that most Northerners didn't have the will to fight.

SHILOH

Just as Northerners were shocked into reality by the First Battle of Bull Run, so too were Southerners by the **Battle of Shiloh**. In April 1862, Union General **Ulysses S. Grant** engaged Confederate forces at Shiloh, Tennessee, in an incredibly bloody battle. Tens of thousands of men died. By the end of the bloodbath, Grant had won and demonstrated to the Confederates that Lincoln was serious about maintaining the Union. Southerners got the message and dug in for a longer war.

ANTIETAM

Rather than wait around for the enemy to attack him, Lee made an aggressive push into the **border states** to try to defeat the Union on its own turf. He also hoped that a Confederate victory in Maryland would convince the state legislature to secede. In September 1862, Lee's army met General **George McClellan**'s troops at the **Battle of Antietam**, which resulted in more than 23,000 casualties—the bloodiest single day of battle of the entire war. Lee was forced to retreat back to Confederate territory.

NEW UNION LEADERSHIP

However, the overly cautious McClellan refused to pursue Lee into Virginia and deliver a fatal blow to the Confederate army. Lincoln was so angry at McClellan for passing up a chance to end the war that he fired McClellan and replaced him with another general. After terminating McClellan, Lincoln had to sift through a couple more generals before he finally settled on **Ulysses S. Grant**, who, unlike McClellan, knew that time was of the essence and that the war could not be allowed to drag on.

THE EMANCIPATION PROCLAMATION

Despite McClellan's failure to follow up, Lincoln nonetheless capitalized on the Antietam victory by issuing the **Emancipation Proclamation** that freed all slaves in the Confederacy. The immediate practical effects of the proclamation were limited: since it declared that slaves only in the secessionist states were free (*not* the **border states**, for Lincoln did not want to provoke them into secession), it was effectively unenforceable.

The proclamation did have a large political impact, though, because it tied the issue of slavery to the restoration of the Union. Indeed, reunification, not emancipation, remained Lincoln's most important goal by far. He once remarked, "If I could save the Union without freeing any slave, I would do it; and if I could save it by freeing all the slaves, I would do it; and if I could do it by freeing some and leaving others alone, I would also do that. What I do about slavery and the colored race, I do because I believe it helps to save this Union." Lincoln received a lot of criticism from the **Peace Democrats** and other groups for wedding the goals of emancipation and reunification.

Despite the priority Lincoln placed on reunification, he knew that a reunified nation would not survive long if slavery still existed. Slavery had been at the root of every major sectional conflict since the 1780s, and the issue had to be addressed. Even though the Emancipation Proclamation failed to ban slavery in the border states, it did mark the symbolic beginning of the end for the "peculiar institution" for every state in the Union.

THE WAR AT SEA

While the armies battled on land, the Union and Confederate navies clashed on the high seas. At the very beginning of the war, Lincoln bypassed Congress and ordered a **naval blockade** of all Southern ports. The South's economy relied almost entirely on cotton trade with Britain, so Lincoln hoped the blockade would strangle the Confederacy financially.

The Confederate navy, though small, proved a formidable adversary. The British-built Confederate warship *Alabama* sank more than sixty Union ships before it was finally defeated. The South also created a major new naval weapon—the **ironclad**—when ingenious Confederate shipbuilders refitted the old warship **USS** *Merrimack* with a steam engine and iron plates to make it impervious to bullets and cannonballs. The ship, renamed the *Virginia*, easily destroyed several Union ships and broke through the blockade. In response,

the Union built an ironclad of its own, the **USS *Monitor***, that fea-
tured an innovative gun turret. The two ships met in March 1862 at
the **Battle of the Ironclads**, which ended in a draw.

GETTYSBURG

Undaunted by his failure at Antietam, Lee marched into Northern
territory again in the summer of 1863, this time into Pennsylvania.
There, he met Union forces at the **Battle of Gettysburg** in early July.
At the end of a bloody three-day struggle in which more than
50,000 died, Lee was once again forced to retreat. The battle was a
resounding victory for the North and a catastrophe for the South.

VICKSBURG

At the same time Lee was losing in the North, Grant was besieging
the city of **Vicksburg**, Mississippi, in the West. Eventually, the
trapped Confederates caved in to Grant's demand for an unconditional surrender. This major victory at the **Battle of Vicksburg** gave
the Union control of the Mississippi River and thus split the Confederacy in half.

THE GETTYSBURG ADDRESS

Lincoln commemorated the Union victory at Gettysburg several
months after the battle with a speech at the dedication of a national
cemetery on the site. Though very brief, the **Gettysburg Address** was
poignant and eloquent. In the speech, Lincoln argued that the Civil
War was a test not only for the Union but for the entire world, for it
would determine whether a nation conceived in democracy could
"long endure."

THE FINAL YEAR: 1864–1865

EVENTS

1864	Grant takes command of Union troops
	Lincoln is reelected
	Sherman begins March to the Sea
1865	Davis proposes Hampton Roads peace conference
	Robert E. Lee surrenders to Grant at Appomattox Courthouse

KEY PEOPLE

Abraham Lincoln 16th U.S. president; overcame significant opposition in the election of 1864 and pursued policy of total war and unconditional surrender

Jefferson Davis President of the Confederacy; struggled to maintain unity among the Southern states; made unsuccessful bid for peace with the North prior to surrender

William Tecumseh Sherman Union general famous for his total war strategy; made devastating March to the Sea from Atlanta to Savannah in 1864

Ulysses S. Grant Union general who defeated Lee's forces and negotiated surrender at Appomattox Court House, Virginia

Robert E. Lee Confederate general who surrendered unconditionally to Grant at Appomattox Court House

George McClellan Former Union general who ran unsuccessfully for president as a Peace Democrat against Lincoln in 1864

SHERMAN'S MARCH TO THE SEA

President **Abraham Lincoln** and General **Ulysses S. Grant** chose to step up the war in 1864 after realizing that limited campaigns against Confederate forces were having little effect. Both knew that the war had to end quickly if the Union were to be restored. Grant therefore ordered his close friend and fellow general **William Tecumseh Sherman** to take a small force through the heart of the Deep South. That summer, Sherman embarked on his now-famous **March to the Sea**, defeated Confederate troops protecting **Atlanta**, Georgia, and then besieged the city. When the citizens of Atlanta failed to surrender, Sherman burned the city and then marched on to **Savannah**. Along the way, he destroyed railroads, burned homes, razed crops, and generally looted and pillaged the entire countryside—one witness said a tornado could not have done more damage. Sherman arrived in Savannah that December and accepted the city's surrender, then marched northward to South Carolina.

LIMITED WAR VS. TOTAL WAR

Prior to 1864, both Union and Confederate commanders had waged a rather **limited war**, with the armies usually fighting only each other, without inflicting damages on innocent civilians or private property. Lincoln, Grant, and Sherman realized, however, that they would have to use a new strategy to end the war, because it was the support of these very same civilians that was keeping the war going in the South. Only when Southern civilians demanded an end to the war would the Confederacy lose its will to fight. As a result, Lincoln, Grant, and Sherman decided to open up a **total war** in which no one was innocent and private property was fair game.

PRESSURE ON LINCOLN

As the fighting dragged on into late 1864, more and more pressure fell on Lincoln to end the war. He came under fire from a growing number of **Peace Democrats** who wanted to strike a deal with the South. Commonly referred to as "Copperheads," after the poisonous snake, these Peace Democrats were particularly numerous in Ohio, Indiana, and Illinois, where there were many Confederate sympathizers. They believed that Lincoln and his generals had shown that they were incapable of restoring the Union, and many were also angry that Lincoln had made the war about slavery and emancipation. From the other side, **Radical Republicans** also attacked Lincoln, claiming that he was not harsh enough on the South.

THE ELECTION OF 1864

Bitterness and uncertainty clouded the **election of 1864**. Despite opposition from the radicals, the **Republican Party** lukewarmly nominated Lincoln for a second term. In a surprise move, Lincoln chose as his running mate Democrat **Andrew Johnson** from the reconquered state of Tennessee, hoping that Johnson would win him votes from prowar Democrats in the North. Together they campaigned on a platform for the South's unconditional surrender. Peace Democrats nominated Lincoln's old foe General **George McClellan**, who wanted peace negotiations and settlement. In the end, Lincoln managed to win 55 percent of the popular vote.

IMPORTANCE OF THE ELECTION

The election of 1864 was crucial because its outcome would determine the entire direction of the war: if Lincoln won, the war would be fought until the South had surrendered unconditionally, but if McClellan won, there would almost surely be a settlement. The election, therefore, was also the Confederacy's last hope for survival. Although Lincoln believed he would lose—even though the Union was finally winning, he thought that most Northerners were against continuation of the war—his reelection ultimately provided a clear mandate to demand **unconditional surrender**.

THE SOUTH'S COLLAPSE

The South, meanwhile, was spiraling into turmoil. The Union naval blockade, Sherman's campaign in Georgia, lack of assistance from Britain, worsening class conflicts, and the collapse of the Southern economy were taking their toll. Thousands were deserting the army, thousands more were going hungry at home, and thousands of slaves were fleeing to Union lines. President **Jefferson Davis** tried desperately to hold the Confederate government together, but none of the states would cooperate. In the final month of the war, the Confederacy grew so desperate that it even began to offer slaves their freedom if they would enlist in the Confederate army.

THE HAMPTON ROADS CONFERENCE

Realizing the end was near, Davis requested peace negotiations in a final attempt to save the South. Lincoln agreed, and delegations from both sides met at the **Hampton Roads Conference** in February 1865. No peace agreement was reached, however, because Lincoln was insistent on the South's unconditional surrender, while Davis demanded full independence.

UNION VICTORY AT APPOMATTOX

In April 1865, **Ulysses S. Grant**'s forces broke through **Robert E. Lee**'s defenses and forced the Confederates to retreat. The Confederate forces burned their capital city, Richmond, behind them as they retreated in order to render it useless to the Union armies. His men malnourished and heavily outgunned, Lee chose to surrender. Several days later, on April 9, 1865, Lee surrendered to Grant formally and unconditionally at **Appomattox Courthouse**, Virginia. Grant accepted the surrender and provided the Southerners food for their march home. Jefferson Davis and other ranking Confederates, meanwhile, had been captured fleeing Virginia. The Civil War was over.

STUDY QUESTIONS & ESSAY TOPICS

Always use specific historical examples to support your arguments.

STUDY QUESTIONS

1. *In your opinion, was the Civil War inevitable? Were the North and the South doomed from the beginning to battle each other eventually over the slavery issue?*

The Civil War was essentially inevitable. Ever since Eli Whitney's invention of the cotton gin in the 1790s, the South had been on a completely different economic and social path from the North. In the 1850s, social and political developments, including the publication of *Uncle Tom's Cabin*, the Fugitive Slave Act, Bleeding Kansas, the *Dred Scott* decision, and John Brown's raid on Harpers Ferry, drove the regions further apart. Although the North and the South tried to reconcile their differences with major political compromises in 1820 and in 1850, both attempts failed.

The cotton gin transformed the slave South completely in the early 1800s, when plantation owners abandoned almost all other crops in favor of the newly profitable cotton. To raise more cotton, planters also purchased more slaves from Africa and the West Indies before the slave trade was banned in 1808. Thousands of blacks were brought into the United States during these years to tend to cotton fields. The size of plantations increased from relatively small plots to huge farms with as many as several hundred slaves each. Because the entire Southern economy became dependent on cotton, it also became dependent on slavery. Although Northern factories certainly benefited indirectly from slavery, Northern social customs were not tied to slavery as Southern customs were.

Events in the 1850s proved that the North-South slavery divide was irreconcilable. Harriet Beecher Stowe's 1852 novel *Uncle Tom's Cabin*, which awakened Northerners to the plight of Southern slaves, became an overnight bestseller in the North but was banned in the South. The book was particularly powerful in the wake of the 1850 Fugitive Slave Act, which forbade both Northerners and Southerners to assist runaway slaves—a law that troubled even those who had shown little sympathy for the abolitionist cause. The "Bleeding Kansas" violence of 1856 between proslavery groups and Free-Soilers shocked people in the North and in the South and demonstrated just how strongly the opposing camps felt about their beliefs. In 1857, the *Dred Scott* decision outraged Northerners because it declared the Missouri Compromise unconstitutional and effectively opened the North to slavery. Finally, John Brown's 1859 raid on Harpers Ferry, Virginia, and subsequent execution proved to be the last straw for many on both sides. Northerners mourned the "martyr" Brown, while Southerners celebrated his death as a great victory. These events of the 1850s convinced Americans in both the North and South that there could be no compromise on the slavery issue.

Both sides had tried to resolve the issue on numerous occasions, but to no avail. The Missouri Compromise of 1820 had established the 36° 30' parallel as the border between the slave states and the free states. This compromise satisfied both sides for a while but eventually became too restrictive for the South. The Compromise of 1850 likewise sought to end the slavery debate after the Mexican War and the Wilmot Proviso raised the question of slavery in the West—but in the end these peaceful resolutions were also unsatisfactory. As a result, in light of the deep political, economic, and social divides, as well as the failure of compromise attempts, armed conflict was thus inevitable.

2.   *Why were the border states so important to Lincoln?*

When South Carolina seceded from the Union in 1860, four of the other fourteen slave states—Maryland, Delaware, Kentucky, and Missouri—chose to remain in the Union rather than join the Confederacy. West Virginia eventually seceded from Virginia in 1863 to become a nonslave state in the Union, too. These five border states were crucial to the North both geographically and economically. As a result, Lincoln was careful to maintain the border states' allegiance and refrained from pursuing any policies that might be too bold and potentially alienating to slave owners in those states. Ultimately, the North's possession of the border states directly affected the outcome of the war.

First and foremost, the border states provided a physical and ideological buffer between the North and South: if Maryland had seceded, Washington, D.C., would have been entirely surrounded by Confederate territory. Lincoln was acutely aware of Maryland's importance: in the spring of 1861, he even turned to military force and instituted martial law in the state to keep it loyal to the Union.

The border states were just as important economically, especially because Maryland and Delaware contained many factories and industrial complexes. Had just those two states joined the Confederacy, they would have doubled the South's manufacturing capability. Lacking these factories, though, the South ended up starving under the Union's naval blockade. Indeed, the Civil War was in many ways an economic war, and doubling Southern manufacturing output could have seriously altered the duration and even the outcome of the conflict.

Finally, the border states' loyalty to the Union showed that slave states had an alternative to secession. The South, for its part, had justified secession by claiming that slave states had to secede to save their "peculiar institution" and their way of life. The fact that the border states—where slavery was practiced—remained in the Union severely weakened this claim.

For all these reasons, Lincoln remained careful not to offend slave owners in the border states. The most notable example of his sensitivity to this issue is the 1863 Emancipation Proclamation, which declared slaves free in only the secessionist states—*not* the loyal border states. Ultimately, Lincoln's measures were effective, and the continued loyalty of the border states was a major factor in the Union's eventual victory.

3.   *Compare the North and the South in 1860 and then again in 1864. Why did the North win the war?*

Although both the North and the South thought they would easily win the Civil War, the South was in many ways doomed from the start. Indeed, by 1864 the South was in ruins, its economy destroyed by blockade, hyperinflation, and the North's campaign of total warfare. In the end, it was the Northern economy and deficiencies in the Southern political system that won and lost the war.

When war broke out in 1861, both sides thought they would win quickly and easily. The Union had experience and international recognition, a robust industrial economy, a strong federal government, twice the population of the South, and twice as many young men for its army. On the other hand, the new Confederacy had cotton (which it believed to be superior to industry), had better military commanders, and believed it could bring Britain into the war on its side. Just as important, however, was the South's feeling of righteousness that followed secession: Southerners felt they were carrying on the tradition of overthrowing tyrannous governments that the founding fathers of the United States had begun. In addition, Southern soldiers, fighting on their home territory, also had an intense desire to fight to protect their homes and families.

By the end of 1864, however, the South lay in ruins, and very little remained of the once-proud Cotton Kingdom. The price of goods was so high and money was so worthless that it cost Southerners in some places several hundred Confederate dollars to buy a single loaf of bread. As a result, hunger and malnutrition became rampant. In addition, much of the landscape from Tennessee to Georgia and up to South Carolina had been razed by General William Tecumseh Sherman's troops on their March to the Sea. Many slaves in the South effectively emancipated themselves by refusing to work and flocking to Union lines in droves. The North, meanwhile, was in many ways better off in 1864 than it had been before the war, for the economy had experienced an enormous boom during the war years and had set the industrial machine into high gear.

This industrial boom in the North, coupled with the Richmond government's inability to provide cohesive leadership, won the war for the Union. Virtually all the effective measures passed by the Union government went unanswered by the Confederacy. Congress in Washington, D.C., for example, stabilized the Northern economy early on in the war by passing the Legal Tender Act, replacing the hundreds of different state and private bank currencies with a single federal dollar. Because this "greenback" currency was supported by the U.S. Treasury, investors knew it was safe and reliable. The National Banking Act also gave the federal government unprecedented control over the banking system and the economy as a whole. The Confederate government, on the other hand, dominated by states' righters, never enacted any such federal laws but instead continued to reserve most powers for the individual states. This inaction, combined with the devastating economic effects of the Union's naval blockade of the South, left the Confederate war effort doomed early on.

Suggested Essay Topics

1. Which side benefited more from the Compromise of 1850, the North or the South?

2. In 1850, most Northerners would never have dreamed they would be fighting a war against the South. Why did Northern public opinion change?

3. Some historians have claimed that the Mexican War was the first battle of the Civil War. Do you agree? Why or why not?

4. What effect did the Bleeding Kansas crisis have on the slavery debate in the years immediately before the war?

5. Compare and contrast Abraham Lincoln and Jefferson Davis as wartime presidents. What challenges did they face and how did they overcome them? Who, in your opinion, was the better leader, and why?

6. What was Britain's role in the Civil War?

7. What was the significance of the Emancipation Proclamation? What effect did it have on the North and on the South?

REVIEW & RESOURCES

QUIZ

1. What did the Wilmot Proviso do?

    A. Banned slavery in the Mexican Cession
    B. Overturned the Missouri Compromise of 1820
    C. Opened Kansas to slaveholding settlers
    D. Applied the doctrine of popular sovereignty to
        settlement of the West

2. Why was the election of 1848 significant?

    A. It marked the first time a Whig won the presidency
    B. It was the first election in which Southern Whigs voted
        with Southern Democrats
    C. The Free-Soilers diverted enough votes from the
        Democrats to let Taylor win
    D. Americans overwhelmingly voted for popular
        sovereignty in the territories

3. All of the following were components of the Compromise of
    1850 *except*

    A. A new Fugitive Slave Law was passed
    B. Slavery was banned in Washington, D.C.
    C. Popular sovereignty would determine the future of
        slavery in the territories
    D. California was admitted as a free state

4. All of the following steeled Northern public opinion against
    the South *except*

    A. The Kansas-Nebraska Act
    B. The Wilmot Proviso
    C. *Uncle Tom's Cabin*
    D. The Fugitive Slave Law

5. Where did Franklin Pierce and his Southern expansionist supporters acquire new territory?

    A. Cuba
    B. Nicaragua
    C. Mexico
    D. Japan

6. Pierce's administration is best described as

    A. Abolitionist and expansionist
    B. Proslavery but conciliatory
    C. Conciliatory and abolitionist
    D. Expansionist and proslavery

7. Why did the Kansas-Nebraska Act anger Americans in the North?

    A. It effectively repealed the Missouri Compromise
    B. It split both the Whig and Democratic Parties
    C. It led to shocking violence in Kansas
    D. It contradicted Southern concessions made in the Compromise of 1850

8. Who were the "border ruffians"?

    A. Ambivalent Americans living in the border states during the Civil War
    B. Proslavery Marylanders who attacked federal troops marching to Washington, D.C., in 1861
    C. Proslavery Missourians who rushed to Kansas after Congress passed the Kansas-Nebraska Act
    D. British troops stationed in Canada who threatened Lincoln with war over the Trent Affair

9. Why did Stephen Douglas push the Kansas-Nebraska Act through Congress in 1854?

  A. He wanted a northern transcontinental railroad to terminate in Chicago
  B. He wanted to resolve the slavery debate
  C. He wanted to increase his stature within the Democratic Party
  D. All of the above

10. John Brown's Pottawatomie Massacre

  A. Was hailed as an abolitionist victory in the North
  B. Began the Bleeding Kansas crisis
  C. Was denounced by most Northerners but lauded by Republicans
  D. All of the above

11. All of the following were consequences of the Kansas-Nebraska Act *except*

  A. The breakup of both the Whig and Democratic Parties
  B. The effective repeal of the Missouri Compromise
  C. The Bleeding Kansas crisis
  D. The Wilmot Proviso

12. The 1857 *Dred Scott v. Sanford* decision prompted

  A. South Carolina to threaten secession
  B. John Brown to kill five proslavery whites in the Pottawatomie Massacre
  C. Border ruffians to burn Lawrence, Kansas
  D. Stephen Douglas to announce the Freeport Doctrine

13. Roger Taney declared the Missouri Compromise unconstitutional on the grounds that

  A. Blacks could not sue in federal courts because they were not citizens
  B. Popular sovereignty was illegal
  C. The federal government could not restrict the movement of private property
  D. Slavery was illegal in both the North and South

14. What statement best describes President James Buchanan's position?

    A.   He supported the South because of his dependency on Southern Democrats

    B.   He supported Northern Democrats in the face of increasing opposition in the South

    C.   He took no stand on the slavery issue in order to get reelected

    D.   He tacitly supported Northern Free-Soilers in exchange for votes

15. All of the following were true about the election of 1860 *except*

    A.   It was primarily a sectional election

    B.   No candidate received a majority of the popular vote

    C.   Lincoln threatened to invade the South after he won

    D.   The Democratic Party split after failing to nominate a single candidate

16. What did Lincoln do in his first inaugural address?

    A.   Threatened to invade the South if the state legislature refused to retract their vote to secede

    B.   Threatened to emancipate all the slaves in the South if more states seceded

    C.   Professed his friendship for the South and said he would ignore South Carolina's illegal secession

    D.   Said he would forgive the South if it emancipated all its slaves

17. In terms of structure, the Confederate government was similar in many ways to

    A.   The Union government

    B.   The U.S. government under the Articles of Confederation

    C.   Britain's parliament

    D.   The Second Continental Congress

REVIEW & RESOURCES

18. What did John Brown's raid on Harpers Ferry demonstrate?

     A. That Southern slaves were not ready to rebel
     B. That Republicans were secretly backing slave insurrections
     C. That the Compromise of 1850 had failed
     D. That Northern and Southern opinions on slavery were irreconcilable

19. What did Stephen Douglas's Freeport Doctrine challenge?

     A. The *Dred Scott v. Sanford* decision
     B. The Wilmot Proviso
     C. The Compromise of 1850
     D. Popular sovereignty

20. Stephen Douglas rejected the Lecompton Constitution on the grounds that

     A. Admitting Kansas as a slave state would violate the Missouri Compromise
     B. Admitting Kansas as a slave state would destroy the sectional balance in the Senate
     C. Kansas could not be admitted without Nebraska
     D. Its drafters had been elected illegitimately

21. What did champions of popular sovereignty believe?

     A. That states should have the final say over the federal government when interpreting the Constitution
     B. That more people, including women and free blacks, should be given the right to vote
     C. That each territory should determine whether it became a free or slave state
     D. That presidents and senators should be directly elected by the people

22. What did Harriet Tubman and other Underground Railroad "conductors" defy?

    A. The Fugitive Slave Law
    B. The Wilmot Proviso
    C. The Tallmadge Amendment
    D. Popular sovereignty

23. Why were the Lincoln-Douglas debates significant in Lincoln's political career?

    A. They won him the Illinois Senate race
    B. They boosted him to national prominence
    C. They ridiculed the untouchable Stephen Douglas
    D. All of the above

24. The seizure of Fort Sumter

    A. Shattered Confederate morale
    B. Convinced Britain to construct the Laird rams
    C. Made Southerners believe the war would be over quickly
    D. Convinced Lincoln to fire General McClellan

25. Why did Southern Democrats refuse to support Stephen Douglas in the election of 1860?

    A. They disagreed with his popular sovereignty platform
    B. He chose a former Free-Soil Party Northerner as his running mate
    C. The South wanted to secede while Douglas wanted to remain in the Union
    D. He had rejected the Lecompton Constitution

26. Britain and the Union almost went to war over

    A. The Laird rams
    B. The Trent Affair
    C. The *Alabama*
    D. All of the above

REVIEW & RESOURCES

27. Which of the following was one reason the border states were so important to the Union?

  A. They would have doubled Confederate manufacturing capabilities had they seceded

  B. The provided Lincoln with the votes he needed to win the election of 1864

  C. They formed an impenetrable defensive shield for the North

  D. The provided the North with slave labor

28. Lincoln was different from Davis in that he

  A. Had more leadership experience prior to the war

  B. Had a knack for understanding and using public opinion to his advantage

  C. Never violated the Constitution

  D. Was unable to control the central government well

29. Which of the following states was *not* a border state?

  A. Kentucky

  B. Maryland

  C. Missouri

  D. Ohio

30. What did the Legal Tender Act do?

  A. Caused the Panic of 1857

  B. Drastically inflated commodity prices in the South

  C. Stabilized the Northern economy

  D. Caused the collapse of the national banking system

31. Why was Britain not as dependent on Southern cotton as the Confederacy had believed?

  A. Britain's economy was shifting away from textile manufacturing

  B. Cotton could also be obtained from Egypt and India

  C. Manufacturers could use wool just as easily as cotton

  D. Most Britons were morally opposed to slavery

32. The Richmond Bread Riots were the result of

    A.   Hyperinflation

    B.   The collapse of the Southern economy

    C.   The North's total warfare tactics

    D.   All of the above

33. What did the Emancipation Proclamation do?

    A.   Freed all slaves in the North and South

    B.   Freed slaves in secessionist states

    C.   Freed only slaves in the border states

    D.   Freed all Southern slaves who volunteered for the Union army

34. William Tecumseh Sherman's March to the Sea

    A.   Was a classic example of total warfare

    B.   Was a classic example of limited warfare

    C.   Forced Robert E. Lee to surrender

    D.   Caused the collapse of the Confederate government in Richmond

35. The Union victory at Antietam was significant because

    A.   It convinced Britain not to forge an alliance with the South

    B.   It gave Lincoln the opportunity to fire George McClellan

    C.   It gave Lincoln the opportunity to issue the Emancipation Proclamation

    D.   All of the above

36. The Battles of Gettysburg and Vicksburg

    A.   Boosted Confederate morale

    B.   Nearly convinced France to extend diplomatic recognition to the South

    C.   Were the major turning point in the war

    D.   Justified Peace Democrats' criticism of Lincoln and the war

REVIEW & RESOURCES

37. Which of the following actions by Lincoln violated the Constitution?

    A. His order of a naval blockade of the South
    B. His increase of the size of the U.S. Army
    C. His authorization of illegal voting methods in the border states
    D. All of the above

38. Why did Lincoln suspend the writ of habeas corpus?

    A. To restrict freedom of the press
    B. To enable Confederate sympathizers to be arrested without being formally charged
    C. To emancipate slaves in Washington, D.C.
    D. To increase the size of the U.S. Army

39. The National Banking Act

    A. Made it easier to obtain cheap credit
    B. Caused a brief financial panic
    C. Gave Congress unprecedented control over the economy
    D. Curbed rampant inflation in the North

40. What did George McClellan and other Peace Democrats want?

    A. To punish the South for causing the Civil War
    B. To end the war and let the South go
    C. To make Kansas a slave state
    D. To fight only a limited war, not a total war, against the South

41. Why did Jefferson Davis request the Hampton Roads Conference with the North?

    A. He knew the Confederacy was doomed
    B. He knew the North was growing weaker and weaker
    C. He wanted to claim that he had tried to make peace with the North
    D. He objected to the North's tactics of total warfare

42. All of the following were Confederate strengths going into the Civil War *except*

    A. Superior military commanders
    B. The fact that it would be fighting a defensive war
    C. A larger population and army
    D. An extensive manufacturing base

43. Toward the end of the war, many poorer whites in the South felt

    A. That they were willing to die for the honor of the South
    B. Angry that they were fighting a rich man's war
    C. That they were close to victory
    D. That Robert E. Lee had failed them

44. All of the following were Northern strengths going into the war *except*

    A. Superior military commanders
    B. A stable and internationally recognized government
    C. A larger population and army
    D. An industrial economy

45. The Confederacy collapsed at the end of the war for all of the following reasons *except*

    A. Hyperinflation
    B. Class struggles
    C. Massive slave uprisings
    D. The federal government's inability to maintain control over the states

46. Lincoln's primary objective during the war was

    A. To free the slaves
    B. To restore the Union
    C. To uphold federal authority over the states
    D. All of the above

REVIEW & RESOURCES

47. What did Harriet Beecher Stowe's novel *Uncle Tom's Cabin* do?

    A. Prompted South Carolina to secede from the Union
    B. Turned many ambivalent Northerners into abolitionists
    C. Convinced many Northerners that reconciliation was possible
    D. Criticized Lincoln for the war

48. The First Battle of Bull Run

    A. Convinced Northerners the war would be over quickly
    B. Convinced Southerners the war would be over quickly
    C. Convinced the North and the South the war would be over quickly
    D. Convinced the North and the South the war would be long and bloody

49. The Battle of Shiloh

    A. Convinced Northerners the war would be long and bloody
    B. Convinced Southerners the war would be long and bloody
    C. Convinced both the North and the South the war would be long and bloody
    D. Convinced the South the war would be over quickly

50. Who won the presidential election of 1864?

    A. James Buchanan
    B. Andrew Johnson
    C. Ulysses S. Grant
    D. Abraham Lincoln

ANSWER KEY

1. A; 2. C; 3. B; 4. B; 5. C; 6. D; 7. A; 8. C; 9. D; 10. B; 11. D; 12. D; 13. C;
14. A; 15. C; 16. C; 17. B; 18. D; 19. A; 20. D; 21. C; 22. A; 23. B; 24. C;
25. D; 26. D; 27. A; 28. B; 29. D; 30. C; 31. B; 32. D; 33. B; 34. A; 35. D;
36. C; 37. D; 38. B; 39. C; 40. B; 41. A; 42. C; 43. B; 44. A; 45. A; 46. B;
47. B; 48. B; 49. B; 50. D

SUGGESTIONS FOR FURTHER READING

DAVIS, WILLIAM C. *"A Government of Our Own": The Making of the Confederacy*. Baton Rouge: Louisiana State University Press, 1994.

FAUST, DREW GILPIN. *Mothers of Invention: Women of the Slaveholding South in the American Civil War*. New York: Vintage, 1996.

GIENAPP, WILLIAM E. *Abraham Lincoln and Civil War America: A Biography*. New York: Oxford University Press, 2002.

MCPHERSON, JAMES. *Battle Cry of Freedom: The Civil War Era*. New York: Oxford University Press, 1988.

———. *The Negro's Civil War: How American Blacks Felt and Acted During the War for the Union*. New York: Vintage, 2003.

STAMPP, KENNETH M. *The Peculiar Institution: Slavery in the Ante-Bellum South*. New York: Vintage, 1989.